SUNI LEE:

A STAR IN THE

SPOTLIGHT

The Journey of a Champion Gymnast

James E. Mount

Suni Lee

All rights reserved. No part of this publication may be reproduced, distributed, or transmitted in any form or by any means, including photocopying, recording, and other electronic or mechanical methods, without prior written permission of the publisher, except incase of briefs quotation embodied in critical reviews and certain other noncommercial uses permitted by copyright law.

Copyright ©James E. Mount2024

Suni Lee

TABLE OF CONTENTS

INTRODUCTION
CHAPTER1: A DREAM TAKES FLIGHT
A New Beginning
The Gymnastics Journey Begins
A Champion's Mindset

CHAPTER2: BALANCING ACT
The Weight of Expectations
Facing Adversity
Finding Joy in the Journey

CHAPTER3: HARD WORK PAYS OFF
The Daily Grind
The Power of Sacrifice
Triumphs and Celebrations

CHAPTER4: THE BIG STAGE
The Road to the National Championships
The Countdown Begins
Stepping Into the Spotlight

CHAPTER5: THE OLYMPIC DREAM
Setting Sights on Tokyo
Trials and Triumphs
Embracing the Olympic Spirit

CHAPTER6: SHINING BRIGHT IN Tokyo

Suni Lee

The Atmosphere of the Games
A Performance for the Ages
The Gold Medal Moment

CHAPTER7:MORE THAN JUST A GYMNAST
A Role Model for Young Athletes
Advocacy and Social Impact
A Lasting Legacy

CHAPTER8: THE ROAD AHEAD
Continuing the Gymnastics Journey
Expanding Her Influence Beyond Gymnastics
Education and Personal Growth

CONCLUSION: THE LEGACY OF SUNI LEE

FUN FACTS ABOUT SUNI LEE

GLOSSARY

INTRODUCTION

Meet Suni Lee

In the world of gymnastics, few names shine as strongly as Suni Lee. Born on October 9, 2002, in St. Paul, Minnesota, Suni's road to becoming a star has been nothing short of incredible. From a young age, she showed remarkable skill, a strong spirit, and an unshakable loyalty to her dreams. But Suni's story is not just about gymnastics; it's about determination, courage, and the power of believing in oneself. Growing up in a close-knit family, Suni was surrounded by love and support. Her parents, Yang and Kui Lee noticed her obvious ability early on. At just six years old, Suni began taking dancing classes. Little did she know that this would be the first step in an amazing trip that would lead her to the biggest stage of all the Olympics. As Suni improved her skills, she met obstacles that would test her drive. Gymnastics is a sport that needs not only physical strength but also mental toughness. Suni's trip was filled with long hours of practice, aches, and times of self-doubt. But each time she fell, she got back up, learning from her mistakes and pushing herself to improve. Suni's love for gymnastics fueled her drive, and her hard work began to pay off as she participated in local and regional contests. Suni's family played an important role in her journey. They cheered her on from the stands, enjoying each success and comforting her during failures. Suni often praises her family for her success, saying that their support gave her the strength to keep going. Her parents made sacrifices, taking her to training classes and events, ensuring she had every chance to shine. As she improved in her gymnastics career, Suni caught the attention of teachers and judges alike. She became known for her amazing ability and unique style. With her mix of ease and power, Suni quickly rose through the ranks, fighting at higher levels and winning awards along the way. Each race brought new difficulties, but Suni faced them with a fierce drive and a smile that lit up the room. By the time she was a teenager, Suni was already a rising star in gymnastics. Her hard work and commitment led her to the top level, where she started racing against some of the best gymnasts in the country. She trained at the famous Midwest Gymnastics Center, where she improved her skills and learned the value of teamwork and kindness. Under the direction of her teachers, Suni grew not only as a dancer but also as a person. As Suni Lee prepared to take her skills to the national stage, her dream of

Suni Lee

playing in the Olympics became more real than ever. The thought of honoring her country filled her with joy and drive. Little did she know, her trip would soon take her to the Tokyo Olympics, where she would win the hearts of millions with her amazing acts. In the pages that follow, we will dive deeper into Suni's life, exploring the successes and obstacles that made her into the winner she is today. From her early days in gymnastics to her memorable Olympic moments, Suni Lee's story is one of inspiration and determination. So, let's begin our journey and discover what it truly means to be a star in the spotlight!

CHAPTER1: A DREAM TAKES FLIGHT

A New Beginning

Suni Lee was born into a family that valued hard work and drive. Growing up in St. Paul, Minnesota, Suni was the youngest of three sisters, and her parents, Yang and Kui Lee taught their girls the value of chasing goals. Suni's early years were filled with love, fun, and a sense of excitement. From a young age, she showed an active spirit that hinted at the athlete she would become. When Suni was just six years old, she found dancing at a neighborhood gym. She was drawn to the bright colors of the mats, the fluid moves of the dancers, and the energy in the air. Her parents put her in classes, trying to turn her abundant energy into something useful. It didn't take long for Suni to fall in love with the sport. She was mesmerized by the flips, turns, and routines that displayed both strength and beauty. In her first class, she looked at the older girls performing incredible skills, and at that moment, she felt a spark sparking within her—a dream was beginning to take flight. Suni's passion and drive quickly set her apart from her friends. She was always the first to arrive at the gym and the last to leave, eager to practice every move and perfect her skills. Her teachers noticed her commitment, often commenting on her natural ability and promise. Suni was determined to learn everything she could, and she approached each training lesson with a sense of joy and interest. This renewed interest not only gave her a physical outlet but also helped her build confidence as she conquered new skills.

As Suni grew in her gymnastics journey, her family became her biggest champions. They attended every match and practice, cheering her on with joy. Suni's folks worked hard to ensure she had the tools and opportunities to achieve. They drove her to the gym every day, combining their busy plans with Suni's responsibilities. Their unflinching support played a crucial role in her growth, urging her to chase her dreams fiercely. However, the road to success was not without its obstacles. Suni faced physical and mental hurdles as she learned new skills. There were days when she felt irritated and disheartened, especially when she struggled with certain moves. But instead of giving up, Suni learned to accept these challenges as part of her journey. With each struggle, she grew more robust, building an attitude that would serve her well in the years to come. Through her early days in gymnastics, Suni began to understand the value of persistence. Each time she fell, she got back up, dusted herself off, and tried again. She learned that success was not only about ability but also about hard work and commitment. This lesson would become a cornerstone of her approach to gymnastics and life.By the time she turned seven, Suni was ready to take the next step in her gymnastics journey. She began participating at local meets, showing the skills she had honed in the gym. With each battle, Suni's excitement grew, and she understood that this was just the beginning of her trip. The thrill of playing in front of an audience and hearing the applause drove her desire even more. Little did she know, this was only the start of an amazing journey that would take her to the highest heights of gymnastics.

The Gymnastics Journey Begins

As Suni Lee continued her journey in gymnastics, her ability became more clear, and she started to gain attention beyond her local gym. She was a natural, easily mixing ease with power. With each challenge, she improved her skills and built her confidence, pushing herself to new heights. At just eight years old, she started participating at the regional level, showing her skills against some of the best young gymnasts in the state. Suni's first big challenge was a key moment in her journey. Nervous yet excited, she stepped onto the mat for her first-floor exercise. The bright lights and cheering crowd were exciting, but Suni focused on her show. As she performed her dance, she felt a rush of energy and joy. The clapping at the end filled her heart with joy, and at that moment, she knew she belonged on the gymnastics stage. Her performances began to earn her notice. Suni regularly placed at the top of her age group, and her teachers were pleased by her determination and hard work. They urged her to take her training to the next level, suggesting she join a competition team. This opportunity was both exciting and frightening. The thought of training more seriously excited Suni, but it also meant more duty and commitment. Suni's parents knew the value of this choice and backed her completely. They were proud of her successes and wanted to provide her with the best chances to succeed. With their support, Suni took the risk and joined the competition team at the Midwest Gymnastics Center, a well-respected training center known for creating top gymnasts. This move would prove to be a turning point in her career. At the gym, Suni found herself surrounded by skilled players who shared her interest. She trained under the direction of experienced teachers who noticed her promise and pushed her to succeed. Training lessons became more serious, with a focus on improving her skills and exercises. Suni accepted the task, driven by her dream of one day playing in the Olympics. In addition to the hard training, Suni learned the value of teamwork and friendship. She made bonds with her teammates, who became her second family. Together, they inspired one another, praised each other's victories, and supported each other through tough times. The ties they formed during long hours in the gym produced a sense of connection that pushed Suni to push herself even further.

However, the journey wasn't without its hurdles. As the competition level grew, so did the pressure. Suni faced hurdles, including illnesses and times of self-doubt. There were times when she questioned her skills, asking if she was strong enough to reach her dreams. But through it all, she learned the importance of perseverance. Suni remembers the support of her family, teachers, and peers, which drove her drive to beat challenges.

With each challenge, Suni continued to shine. She won awards and honors, her hard work paying off in real ways. The thrill of standing on the stage, hearing the national song, and praising her successes filled her with pride. As she set her thoughts on the future, Suni knew that her trip was just starting. Each step forward brought her closer to her final dream: playing in the Olympics.

Suni Lee

A Champion's Mindset

As Suni Lee improved in her gymnastics career, she formed a champion's mindset—one that would be important for her success. Gymnastics is not just a physical sport; it takes mental strength, attention, and an upbeat attitude. Suni learned early on that developing the right attitude was just as important as learning her practices.

One of the key aspects of Suni's attitude was her ability to set goals. She began by setting small, realistic goals during training, such as learning a particular skill or improving her score in tournaments. These goals kept her focused and helped her to track her growth. As she achieved each goal, her confidence grew, and she set her goals on bigger tasks. Visualization became another strong tool in Suni's mental toolkit. She learned to picture herself performing her moves perfectly in her mind before going onto the mat. This method helped her prepare mentally for events, lowering nervousness and improving her confidence. Suni would close her eyes and imagine the crowd clapping, her teachers smiling with pride, and her friends backing her. This mental practice helped her to enter events with a sense of calm and drive.

Suni also realized the value of keeping an upbeat mood, even in the face of hardship. There were times when she faced setbacks, whether it was a poor showing or a difficult exercise day. Instead of focusing on negative thoughts, she practiced thankfulness, telling herself how far she had come and the support she had gotten from her family and teachers. This mindset change helped her bounce back stronger and more driven than ever.

Support from her family and teachers played a vital role in supporting Suni's winning attitude. They urged her to accept difficulties, telling her that failing is a part of the journey. With their unshakable belief in her skills, Suni learned to view failures as chances for growth rather than insurmountable hurdles. This viewpoint change helped her to approach her training with grit and drive. As Suni continued to participate, she found that the mental side of gymnastics was just as important as physical training. She created practices to handle her jitters before events, including deep breathing exercises and positive statements. These habits helped her stay focused and calm, allowing her to perform at her best when it meant most. The road to becoming a great dancer was not easy, but Suni accepted

Suni Lee

the challenges with an unwavering spirit. Her commitment to her work, paired with a champion's attitude, set her apart from her peers. Suni Lee was not just a skilled dancer; she was a young woman eager to achieve her dreams. With each passing day, she got closer to her goal of making it to the Olympic stage, armed with the idea that anything was possible through hard work and determination.

CHAPTER2: BALANCING ACT

The Weight of Expectations

As Suni Lee went deeper into her gymnastics journey, she faced the truth of demands. The joy of competition came with its pressures—pressure from teachers, friends, and even herself. While she thrived in the spotlight, Suni quickly learned that the road to success was not only about love but also about handling the weight of demands that often felt heavy on her shoulders.

In the early stages of her professional career, Suni loved the thrill of playing and the joy of learning new skills. However, as she moved up the ranks, the risks became higher. Competitions were no longer just fun events; they were chances to show themselves against the best in the country. The desire to succeed and please her teachers and family weighed on her, causing times of worry that were difficult to shake. Suni found herself questioning her skills, wondering if she could meet the standards set before her. To deal with these thoughts, Suni learned the value of conversation. She reached out to her teachers and family, sharing her ideas and worries. This openness allowed her to share her fears, easing some of the pressure she felt. Her teachers told her that standards should inspire, not overpower. They urged her to focus on her progress rather than simply on results. This change in viewpoint helped Suni find her balance amid the pressures of professional gymnastics. In addition to conversation, Suni created coping techniques to handle her stress. She added awareness practices into her training routine, including deep breathing routines and meditation methods. These routines helped her stay centered and focused, allowing her to approach contests with a clear mind. Instead of being consumed by the fear of failure, Suni learned to put her energy into achieving her best.

As she managed these difficulties, Suni found the value of self-compassion. She understood that everyone experiences ups and downs and that it is okay to have times of self-doubt. Embracing her flaws helped her to approach her training with a sense of ease and understanding. Rather than being tough on herself for mistakes, she learned to enjoy her growth and realize the hard work she had put in. The love of her family stayed a constant source of strength. Suni's parents always told her that they loved her wholeheartedly, regardless of her results. Their constant belief in her skills helped her develop confidence and resilience. She learned that her worth was not simply defined by awards or points but by her love for gymnastics and the joy it brought her.

Through this path of facing obstacles and controlling expectations, Suni found a better knowledge of her love for gymnastics. It was not just about winning; it was about the love of the sport and the bonds she built along the way. By accepting her journey and focusing on personal growth, Suni learned to handle the challenges of professional gymnastics while staying true to herself.

Facing Adversity

As Suni Lee continued to rise through the ranks of gymnastics, she met her fair share of hardship. Each setback offered a chance for growth, teaching her important lessons about resiliency and drive. Suni's ability to face hardship head-on would shape her into the winner she was meant to become. One of the most important hurdles Suni faced was an illness that threatened her growth. While training for an upcoming competition, she fell awkwardly during a routine and felt a sharp pain in her ankle. Concerned, her teachers quickly assessed the situation, and it was decided that she would need to take time off to heal. This news hit Suni hard; she was heartbroken at the thought of missing events and letting her team down. During her healing, Suni dealt with anger and self-doubt. She missed the thrill of performance and the friendship of her coworkers. However, instead of submitting to negative, Suni focused on her recovery. She worked closely with her physical trainer, following a strict routine to strengthen her ankle and regain her confidence. Suni learned the value of patience during this time, knowing that healing was a process that needed time and effort.

Throughout her healing, Suni also learned the importance of mental strength. She participated in meditation methods, imagining herself back on the mat and completing her exercises perfectly. This mental practice kept her feelings high and reminded her of her love for gymnastics. With each passing day, Suni grew stronger, both physically and mentally. She returned to the gym with a renewed resolve, eager to show to herself that she could beat this barrier. Suni's road through hardship went beyond physical obstacles. As she faced the pressures of competition, she met times of self-doubt. Competing against top dancers in her age group often led her to compare herself to others. She would sometimes question whether she was good enough to succeed. During these times, Suni learned to remember her successes and the hard work she had put in. Instead of focusing on similarities, she focused on her unique journey and the progress she had made. The support of her family, friends, and teachers played a key part in helping Suni manage challenges. They reminded her of her abilities and urged her to accept obstacles as chances for growth. Their unwavering belief in her skills provided Suni with the support she needed to keep pushing forward, even when the going got tough. Through these events, Suni gained a better knowledge of perseverance. She learned that failures are a normal part of any journey and that the way one reacts to hardship is what truly defines them. Each challenge she faced became a stepping stone, bringing her closer to her goals.

Suni's drive to rise above her challenges drove her love for gymnastics and solidified her identity as a winner.

Finding Joy in the Journey

Amid the hurdles and stresses of professional gymnastics, Suni Lee found the importance of finding joy in her journey. While the goal of success was a major part of her life, it was her love for the sport and the events along the way that drove her drive. Suni learned that gymnastics was not just about prizes and medals; it was about the memories she made, the bonds she forged, and the joy of simply doing what she loved. As Suni trained hard, she made it a point to enjoy every moment in the gym. From the laughter shared with friends to the pleasure of achieving a tough skill, Suni focused on the positive parts of her training. She found joy in the friendship of her team, often participating in friendly joking and praising each other's successes. These times of connection made the hard work feel useful and produced a setting where everyone grew together. Suni also tried to bring fun into her training. She and her friends often played games during practice to lighten the mood and reduce stress. These fun times told her that gymnastics was not just a job; it was a hobby that brought people together. By finding fun in the process, Suni was able to approach her training with a renewed sense of excitement and drive.Moreover, Suni acquired a deep respect for the beauty of gymnastics itself. She looked at the beauty of routines, the ease of moves, and the thrill of dancing in front of an audience. Suni understood that each act told a story, and she wanted her shows to connect with others. This artistic viewpoint helped her to connect with her sport on a deeper level, driving her love and creativity. The love for gymnastics went beyond the competition floor. Suni found joy in sharing her interest with younger dancers at her gym. She often offered to help train younger players, sharing her knowledge and experience. This job not only allowed her to give back to the sport she loved but also reminded her of her own journey. Seeing the excitement in the eyes of younger gymnasts renewed her love, as she thought about the joy she felt when she first started. As Suni accepted the idea of finding joy in the process, she became more strong in the face of difficulties. The pressure of competition became less overwhelming when she focused on her love for gymnastics rather than the result. This change in viewpoint altered her approach to training and competition. Instead of viewing every event as a make-or-break moment, she saw them as chances to showcase her hard work and passion. Suni's fresh viewpoint helped her to succeed in her gymnastics career. She faced events with confidence, joy, and a sense of thanks for the experiences she had gained. The thrill of performance became a party rather than a source of stress. Suni understood that the trip was just as important as the goal, and this understanding fueled her desire to continue chasing her dreams.

CHAPTER 3: HARD WORK PAYS OFF

The Daily Grind

For Suni Lee, success in gymnastics was not merely a product of ability; it was the result of constant hard work, commitment, and a strict training routine. From a young age, Suni understood that achieving her dreams would take sacrifices and an unwavering commitment to her work. The daily grind of training became a way of life, turning her into the athlete she wanted to be.

Suni's workout routine was no regular plan. It was filled with early mornings and late nights, often starting before the sun rose. Waking up while the world was still asleep became second nature to her. She would arrive at the gym with a determined spirit, ready to put in the work necessary to improve her skills. Each day, her routine consisted of fitness exercises, flexibility training, and improving her routines on different equipment, including the balance beam, uneven bars, floor exercise, and vault. To Suni, every part of her training mattered. Conditioning lessons worked on building strength and endurance, while flexibility drills helped her achieve the amazing range of motion needed for her routines. Suni pushed herself to the limit, often feeling tired, but she knew that this effort was important for her growth as a dancer. Her teachers created special workouts suited to her needs, stressing skill and performance. The attention to detail in her training helped her build a strong base in gymnastics, allowing her to master increasingly tough skills. Balancing her school duties with her training was another problem Suni faced. She was a student first and foremost, and controlling her time successfully was important. Suni often found herself doing homework in the car on the way to the gym or studying between training sessions. It wasn't always easy, but she learned the value of focus and time management. Suni's dedication to her schooling and her sport showed her desire to succeed in both areas.

The sacrifices Suni made went beyond her time and energy. She often missed out on social events, such as birthday parties and trips with friends. While her friends enjoyed carefree weekends, Suni was committed to her training, realizing that each missed chance brought her closer to her goals. Though it was difficult at times, Suni kept a positive attitude, telling herself of the bigger picture and the goals she was working toward. Despite the busy routine, Suni found joy in the grind. She valued the ties she made with her friends, who became her second family. Their shared experiences, problems, and victories formed a bond that made the hard work feel valuable. Together, they enjoyed each small win, whether it was learning a new skill or successfully finishing a difficult exercise. These times of friendship kept Suni inspired and drove her love for gymnastics. Suni's commitment to training also paid off in practical ways. As she progressed, she began to see gains in her skills and abilities. Competitions became a platform for her hard work, and with each good act, her confidence grew. The thrill of performing her skills perfectly in front of an audience solidified her love for the sport and pushed her to keep pushing her limits.

Through the daily grind of training, Suni learned that hard work truly pays off. Each drop of sweat and moment of sacrifice brought her one step closer to her dreams. This understanding laid the base for her continued success and instilled in her the belief that patience and determination were key ingredients to achieving greatness.

The Power of Sacrifice

In the world of professional gymnastics, suffering is an essential part of the trip, and for Suni Lee, it was a crucial aspect of her success. Every decision she made was led by her commitment to her sport, and she quickly learned that achieving her goals required giving up certain comforts and experiences. While the sacrifices were difficult, they eventually turned her into the winner she wanted to be. Suni's trip required a large investment of time and energy. Training hours often stretched beyond the normal school day, with routines lasting several hours, five or six days a week. This strict plan meant that Suni had to make tough choices about how she spent her time. While her friends enjoyed sleepovers, movies, and relaxing weekends, Suni committed her weekends to hard training practices and events. This devotion meant missing out on many social meetings and family events, but Suni knew that her love for gymnastics came with its trade-offs.

Additionally, Suni had to be strict with her food and living choices. Nutrition played a vital role in her training routines, and she learned to make better food choices that would feed her body for top performance. While her friends delighted in treats and fast food, Suni focused on healthy meals rich in fruits, veggies, lean meats, and whole carbs. It wasn't always easy to say no to her favorite snacks, but she knew that keeping her health and energy was important for her success.

The mental part of giving was equally difficult. Suni faced times of self-doubt and fear of failing, especially when the pressure to perform was high. The desire to succeed sometimes led to crushing feelings of worry, as she wanted to live up to the standards of her teachers, family, and herself. In these times, Suni learned to accept her weaknesses, realizing that they were a part of her journey. Instead of shying away from obstacles, she chose to face them head-on, using her fears as fuel to work harder.

Through it all, Suni found strength in her support system. Her family played a key part in helping her handle the adjustments she made. They understood her passion for gymnastics and pushed her to follow her dreams completely. Suni's parents were her biggest fans, watching every tournament and praising her successes, no matter how small. Their unwavering belief in her skills boosted her confidence and told her that her sacrifices were valuable.

Suni also connected with her friends, who shared similar experiences and sacrifices. Together, they made a caring group, knowing the unique obstacles each faced on their paths to success. This link created an environment where they could support and boost one another, helping to ease the loneliness that sometimes followed their efforts. They praised each other's successes and offered comfort during tough times, supporting the idea that they were all on this trip together.

As Suni continued to grow as a dancer, she learned to view sacrifice as a stepping stone toward her dreams. The hard work and commitment she put into her training were not just hurdles but important components of her trip. Each sacrifice she made, whether big or small, added to her growth and success. Suni began to enjoy the results of her work, knowing that the sacrifices were not in vain. They were opening the way for her success and turning her into a well-rounded athlete.

In the face of difficulties and sacrifices, Suni Lee emerged stronger, tougher, and more driven than ever. She learned that hard work, when paired with sacrifice and determination, eventually leads to success. With each challenge, she brought the lessons of her sacrifices with her, knowing that they were essential to her journey as a great dancer.

Suni Lee

Triumphs and Celebrations

Suni Lee's journey in gymnastics was not solely marked by hard work and sacrifices; it was also defined by victorious moments that praised her dedication and resilience. Each win, whether big or small, served as a reminder of her progress and the dreams she had worked hard to achieve. Suni's successes became milestones that pushed her forward, driving her desire and inspiring her to reach even greater heights.

As Suni improved her skills and fought at different levels, she began to see the effects of her hard work. One of her earlier wins came when she qualified for a famous gymnastics competition. The thrill and nerves raced within her as she prepared to perform her skills in front of an audience. Stepping onto the mat, Suni focused on the countless hours of practice and training that led her to this moment. With every flip and twist, she put her heart into her act, and when she finished, the thunderous praise rang in her ears. The joy she felt in that moment solidified her love for gymnastics and pushed her to keep aiming for greatness. As she continued to participate, Suni experienced the thrill of standing atop the stage, getting awards and praise for her accomplishments. The first time she won a gold award was a memorable event. The feelings of joy, pride, and amazement washed over her as she listened to the national song play in her honor. This moment was a result of her hard work, sacrifices, and unshakable dedication to her sport. It served as a strong reminder that every early morning and late night in the gym had been worth it. With each competition, Suni grew more confident in her skills, pushing herself to take on new tasks and exercises. She sought to improve with every act, aiming for perfection while accepting the idea that mistakes were chances for growth. This attitude helped her to approach events with a sense of freedom and joy. The fear of failure changed into a desire to showcase her ability, and Suni thrived in the attention.Suni's victories were not limited to individual acts. The ties she made with her friends also became a source of joy. Together, they honored each other's victories, creating an environment of support and encouragement. The joy of winning a team competition, with all members adding to the general success, brought a sense of unity that made the wins even sweeter. These times of joint success showed the importance of teamwork and the strength that came from working together toward a shared goal.Beyond the gym, Suni's successes resonated with her family and neighborhood. Her successes encouraged young gymnasts, showing them what was possible through hard work and commitment. Suni accepted her role as a role model, often visiting local clubs and sharing her story with hopeful athletes. Hearing their dreams and goals sparked a sense of pride in her own journey, and Suni relished the chance to inspire the next generation of gymnasts.

CHAPTER4: THE BIG STAGE

The Road to the National Championships

Suni Lee's trip to the National Championships was a testament to her unwavering drive and relentless chase of greatness. It all started with countless hours of training in the gym, where Suni worked hard to perfect her skills and practices. The road to this elite competition was not easy, but every step along the way prepared her for the difficulties she would face.

The National Championships was a dream that Suni had set her eyes on for years. To qualify for this top event, she had to participate in a number of regional events, showing her ability against some of the best dancers in the country. The stakes were high, and the pressure was obvious. Each fight was a stepping stone, testing her skills and grit as she faced off against tough opponents.

Suni started the competition season with a sense of joy mixed with nerves. She knew that every routine she did would be examined by judges and onlookers alike. The thought of fighting at such a high level pushed her to train harder, focused on improving her skills and executing her routines with precision. The pressure to achieve weighed heavily on her, but Suni viewed it as a chance to show herself.

As the regional events unfolded, Suni faced both successes and difficulties. There were times of joy when she performed her acts perfectly, getting high scores and praise from the judges. These wins boosted her confidence and strengthened her belief in her skills. However, there were also times of sadness. Mistakes in routines or falls during shows reminded her of the uncertain nature of gymnastics and the importance of resiliency.

One of the most important events on her trip was the regional qualifying event, where gymnasts vied for a chance to earn a spot at the National Championships. Suni arrived at the place, her heart racing with expectation. The mood was exciting, filled with the energy of players and fans. Suni took a deep breath, telling herself of the countless hours of planning that had led her to this moment.

With each event, Suni poured her heart and soul into her acts. The balance beam, uneven bars, floor exercise, and vault were not just exercises; they were examples of her commitment and love for the sport. As she stepped onto the mat, she felt a rush of energy, driving her desire to highlight her ability. The audience's cheers and support became a driving force, pushing her to give her best effort.

After an intense battle filled with ups and downs, Suni's hard work and determination paid off. She won a prized spot at the National Championships, marking a major milestone in her gymnastics journey. The moment she got the news was a mix of joy and confusion. The long hours of training, the sacrifices made, and the difficulties faced had resulted in this amazing success. Suni knew that she was one step closer to achieving her dreams.

The road to the National Championships was not just about the goal; it was about the trip itself. Along the way, Suni learned important lessons about resilience, drive, and the value of believing in herself. Each challenge turned her into the dancer she was becoming, giving her a sense of confidence that would serve her well on the big stage.

With her eyes set on the National Championships, Suni was eager to make her mark. The trip had taught her that hard work and commitment could lead to amazing chances. As she prepared for the biggest fight of her life, Suni welcomed the challenges ahead with an unshakable spirit and a desire to present her skills.

The Countdown Begins

As the National Championships came, joy and anticipation filled the air for Suni Lee. It was the moment she had been working toward for years—a chance to fight against the best dancers in the country on a big stage. The countdown started, and with it came a rush of feelings, from joy to nerves. Suni was ready to accept the task ahead.

In the weeks running up to the finals, Suni increased her exercise. Every practice became a chance to perfect her routines, fine-tuning each part to ensure that she performed at her absolute best. Her trainers stressed the importance of regularity and performance, pushing her to keep focus as the competition drew nearer. Suni knew that this was an important moment in her gymnastics career, and she wanted to make every second count. Suni's daily training lessons were filled with hard work and devotion. She woke up early, her mind focused on the upcoming challenge. The gym became her second home, where she felt both pushed and motivated. Each day, she practiced not only her routines but also visualization methods, imagining herself performing each move perfectly. This mental planning became a vital part of her training, helping her build confidence and endurance.

As the countdown continued, Suni faced a storm of feelings. She experienced excitement about the chance to fight on such a famous stage, but she also felt the weight of demands. The pressure to perform well was great, and self-doubt came in at times. Would she be able to deliver under such scrutiny? To fight these thoughts, Suni depended on her support system—her family, teachers, and peers. They told her of her hard work and talents, pushing her to focus on what she could control.

In the final week running up to the National Championships, Suni participated in a planned tapering phase. This meant lowering the volume of her training to allow her body to heal and be at its peak for the race. While this was a nice change, it also came with its own set of difficulties. The quick drop in training intensity left her feeling nervous. She worried that she might lose her edge. However, her trainers told her that this was an important part of planning for the big day. It was time to believe in her training and allow her body to rest. The joy in the gymnastics community was obvious as the National Championships got closer. Suni followed the talk on social media, watching videos of other dancers training for the challenge. She felt motivated by their commitment, but she also had to tell herself to stay focused on her trip. A comparison could easily lead to self-doubt, so Suni focused on her strengths and the unique skills she brought to the floor. On the day before the tournaments, Suni met with her friends for a final drill. The spirit was electric as they shared laughs and support.

Suni Lee

This practice served as a reminder that they were in this together, encouraging each other through the highs and lows. Suni admired the bonds she had made with her coworkers, knowing they were all striving toward their individual goals while also celebrating each other's wins. As night fell, Suni prepared for bed, knowing that the following day would be a turning point in her gymnastics path. She imagined her routines one last time, imagining herself going onto the floor with ease. With a heart full of hope and joy, Suni drifted off to sleep, thinking of the bright lights and screaming crowd that awaited her at the National Championships. The timer had come to an end, but Suni's trip was just starting. With the drive in her heart and a love for gymnastics, she was ready to accept the big stage and present the incredible ability she had worked so hard to build.

Suni Lee

Stepping Into the Spotlight

The day of the National Championships had finally come, and for Suni Lee, it was a moment she had envisioned countless times. As she stood backstage, waiting for her turn to fight, a mix of feelings rushed through her—excitement, nervousness, and a sense of purpose. This was the result of years of hard work and commitment, and Suni was ready to shine.
As she prepared to step onto the mat, Suni took a moment to collect herself. She focused on her breaths, slowing her rushing heart. With each deep breath, she reminded herself of the countless hours of training that had led her to this place. She had trained for this moment, and now it was time to showcase her skills to the world. The bright lights and the expectation of the crowd only boosted her energy. When her

name was called, Suni stepped out onto the floor with confidence. The arena was buzzing with energy as the crowd cheered, and Suni felt the warmth of their support surrounding her. She knew that this was her moment to shine, and she accepted it completely. As she began her routine, every move felt exciting. The floor became her medium, and she danced with ease and accuracy, completing each skill with confidence.

Suni's dances were a mix of beauty and speed, showing her unique style and ability. She had worked hard to improve her routines, and it showed. With every flip, twist, and landing, Suni felt the thrill of acting at her best. The cheers of the crowd inspired her, pushing her to give it her all. She smiled as she heard the clapping, feeding off the energy of the crowd. This was what she loved—the thrill of participating and sharing her passion for gymnastics with others.After finishing her floor exercise, Suni moved to the balance beam, one of the most difficult platforms. The beam needed not only physical skill but also mental focus and calm. As she approached the beam, Suni felt a rush of drive. She had faced countless difficulties with this equipment during practice, but she had also overcome them. This was her time to shine, and she was ready to show the judges and the public what she could do. With steady resolve, Suni performed her dance with ease, showing her strength and poise. Each flip and turn on the narrow beam showed her amazing control and balance. As she dismounted, the crowd burst into praise, and Suni felt a wave of relief and joy. She knew she had given her all, and that was what mattered most.

The final event was the uneven bars, where Suni's skills truly shone. She flew through the air with ease, displaying her strength and skill. The thrill of playing in front of

CHAPTER 5: THE OLYMPIC DREAM

Setting Sights on Tokyo

As Suni Lee's star continued to rise in the world of gymnastics, the dream of playing in the Olympics became a driving force in her life. With the 2020 Tokyo Olympics on the horizon, Suni realized that this was the peak of physical achievement—a chance to serve her country and showcase her skills on the biggest stage in sports. The road toward this renowned event would be filled with obstacles, sacrifices, and the relentless chase of greatness.

Suni Lee

From a young age, Suni had dreams of becoming an Olympic dancer. The Olympics represented the conclusion of years of hard work, commitment, and desire. Watching previous Olympians perform motivated her, sparking a fire within her to reach for greatness. As she moved through her gymnastics career, that dream started to feel more possible, especially after her success at the National Championships. With the Olympics in sight, Suni knew that her training routine would need to become even more intense and focused. She and her teachers created a thorough plan to prepare her physically and emotionally for the difficulties ahead. This training included not only improving her skills but also increasing her strength, flexibility, and endurance. Suni welcomed the stress of her training sessions, knowing that every drop of sweat was a step closer to her Olympic dream.

Suni Lee

In addition to physical training, mental preparedness became crucial. Suni began working with sports coaches to create methods to handle the stresses of competition. The mental part of gymnastics is just as important as the physical, and Suni wanted to ensure she was mentally prepared to perform at her best when it meant most. Visualization techniques became a vital part of her routine, allowing her to mentally practice her acts and build faith in her skills. The trip to Tokyo was not just about individual success; it was also about teamwork. Suni trained alongside her friends, building strong bonds as they worked together to achieve their Olympic goals. They encouraged one another through the highs and lows of training, sharing both victories and failures. This friendship produced a sense of unity, driving their combined desire to succeed as a team.

Suni Lee

As the countdown to the Olympics continued, Suni faced an array of obstacles. Injuries, tiredness, and the pressure of expectations tried her determination. However, she stayed focused on her goal, telling herself that failures were a normal part of the trip. Each task served as a chance to grow stronger and more durable. Suni drew motivation from her family, teachers, and fellow gymnasts, whose constant support inspired her to push through tough times.
In the final months leading up to the Olympics, Suni increased her training, joining different events to gain experience and showcase her skills. These events allowed her to judge her growth and make any necessary changes to her practices. The risks were high, but Suni welcomed the pressure, viewing each event as a stepping stone toward her Olympic dream The expectation of the Tokyo Olympics filled the air

as Suni prepared for the most important challenge of her life. She imagined herself standing on the platform, representing the United States with joy. With her thoughts set on the final goal, Suni stayed committed to her training, knowing that every moment spent in the gym brought her closer to achieving her Olympic dream.

Trials and Triumphs

As Suni Lee continued her training for the 2020 Tokyo Olympics, she faced a number of trials and successes that tested her grit and drive. The road to the Olympics was not just about improving routines and training harder; it was also about beating hurdles and accepting the challenges that came her way.

One of the most important trials came during the Olympic trials, where Suni would fight for a prized spot on the U.S. Olympic gymnastics team. The pressure was great, as only a select few would win the chance to serve their country on the world stage. Suni started the trials with a mix of joy and nerves, fully aware of the risks involved. The trials were a conclusion of all her hard work and planning, and she was determined to rise to the moment.

The mood at the tryouts was exciting. Gymnasts from across the country met, each hoping for a chance to shine. Suni knew she had to perform her best, and she focused on performing her moves with accuracy and confidence. As she stepped onto the floor for her first event, she took a deep breath, telling herself to trust in her training. With each trick she did, Suni felt a rush of energy, the crowd's cheers pushing her forward.

However, the trials also offered new difficulties. During her performance on the balance beam, Suni faced a moment of doubt that almost led to a fall. It was a key time that could have derailed her performance. But in that split second, Suni drew upon her training and mental readiness. She returned her poise and finished the exercise with ease, getting praise from the crowd. This event taught her the value of resiliency and the ability to change under pressure.

As the trials continued, Suni faced additional difficulties, including injuries that threatened to hinder her performance. There were days when tiredness set in, and questions crept into her mind. Despite these hurdles, Suni refuses to give up. She leaned on her support system—her family, teachers, and teammates—who urged her to keep going forward. They told her that every failure was a chance for growth and that she had the strength to beat hardship.

In the face of these trials, Suni also experienced times of success. Her acts won her high marks and praise from experts, proving her hard work and commitment. With each great act, Suni's confidence grew. She felt the thrill of playing at her best and the excitement of being one step closer to achieving her Olympic dream. The cheers of the crowd became a driving force, sparking her love for gymnastics even further.

As the final day of the trials came, Suni knew that the competition was tough, but she stayed focused on her goals. The stakes were bigger than ever, and the pressure was obvious. With each passing moment, she told herself that she had come too far to turn back now. The Olympic dream was within reach, and Suni was ready to take the chance.

When the news came, and Suni learned that she had won a spot on the U.S. Olympic gymnastics team, the feelings rushed over her. Joy, relief, and pride filled her heart as she understood that all her hard work had paid off. She was going to the Olympics! This success was not just a personal win; it was a testament to her grit and drive in the face of hardship.

The struggles and successes of her trip had shaped Suni into the gymnast she had become. Each task had taught her important lessons about determination, strength, and the value of believing in herself. As she prepared for the next part of her Olympic journey, Suni took with her the knowledge that she could beat anything that came her way.

Suni Lee

Embracing the Olympic Spirit

As Suni Lee finally became a part of the U.S. Olympic gymnastics team, she was filled with a feeling of pride and joy. The realization of her Olympic dream was both exciting and humble. However, this success also came with the weight of duty and demands. Suni knew that she was not only promoting herself but also her country and all the young athletes who looked up to her. In the months running up to the Olympics, Suni submerged herself in the Olympic spirit. She learned about the ideals of the Olympics—excellence, respect, and friendship. These ideas rang deeply with her and shaped her approach to competition. Suni understood that the Olympics were not just about getting trophies; they were about praising the commitment and hard work of players from around the world. Suni welcomed the chance to connect with her fellow friends and players from different sports. The unity among the Olympic players was obvious, creating an environment of support and encouragement. Suni engaged in team-building events, sharing stories and experiences with her coworkers. This bond created a sense of unity, telling her that they were all on this trip together.

As the Olympics came, Suni worked on keeping her physical and mental well-being. The pressure of fighting on such a big stage could be exhausting, so she made a conscious effort to value self-care. This included engaging in quiet techniques, getting enough rest, and filling her body with healthy foods. Suni knew that taking care of her mental health was just as important as her physical training. The lead-up to the Tokyo Olympics also offered unique difficulties due to the current pandemic. Health and safety measures were in place, and the mood was different from earlier Olympic games. However, Suni stayed positive, viewing these difficulties as chances for growth. She learned to adapt to the circumstances, finding joy in the times spent with her peers and the shared excitement of honoring their country. As the day of her first Olympic event drew closer, Suni thought about her experience. She thought about the sacrifices she had made and the help she had gotten along the way. This moment was not just about her success; it was a culmination of the dreams and goals of everyone who had believed in her. Suni was motivated to respect that support by giving her best effort.

On the day of her challenge, Suni stepped onto the mat with a heart full of thanks and a spirit ready to shine. The roar of the crowd energized her, and she felt an overwhelming feeling of pride in honoring her country. Suni knew that regardless of the result, she had already achieved something amazing by making the Olympics. As she prepared to perform, Suni accepted the Olympic spirit, focusing on her love for gymnastics and the joy of participating. This moment was a celebration of her hard work and commitment, and she was ready to present her skills to the world. Suni knew that the Olympics were more than just a battle; they were a celebration of the human spirit, perseverance, and the chase of dreams.

CHAPTER 6: SHINING BRIGHT IN Tokyo

The Atmosphere of the Games

As the Tokyo 2020 Olympics developed, the mood was unlike any other. The city, known for its lively culture and cutting-edge technology, was buzzing with excitement. Even with the difficulties brought on by the global pandemic, the spirit of the Olympics showed strongly, attracting athletes and fans alike. For Suni Lee, this was a time she had dreamed of for years, and now she was about to step onto the world stage. The opening event set the tone for the Games, having a beautiful show of Japanese culture and the healing power of sport. Although onlookers were limited due to health rules, the athletes felt the electric energy of their fellow rivals. They were all there to showcase their hard work and commitment, to enjoy their trips, and to fight for fame. Suni stood among her teammates, feeling a sense of unity and pride that came with serving her country on such a prestigious stage.

As the gymnastics events started, the expectations built. The arena was filled with athletes, teachers, and officials, each eager to watch the amazing ability that would unfold. For Suni, the roar of the crowd and the cheers of her fellow rivals drove her drive. She had spent years training for this moment, and she was ready to shine. The stakes were high, but Suni welcomed the pressure, focusing on the joy of acting and showing her skills.

The COVID-19 pandemic had changed the environment of the Olympics in many ways, but it also created a sense of resolve among the athletes. They knew the value of their jobs as symbols of hope and strength. Suni took motivation from her friends, realizing that they were all handling this unique trip together. The support and advice she got from her peers boosted her confidence, telling her that she was not alone in her quest for Olympic fame.

In the days running up to her events, Suni immersed herself in the Olympic spirit. She took time to tour the town and meet with other athletes, learning about their experiences and stories. Each exchange increased her respect for the Olympic community and the shared journey of every participant. Suni felt a sense of connection and strength, knowing that she was part of something bigger than herself.

As her competition day came, Suni kept her focus and drive. She used visualization methods to mentally practice her routines, imagining every step with accuracy and ease. The pressure was great, but Suni understood that this was the moment she had trained for. She was ready to accept the task and present her ability to the world.

When the day finally arrived, Suni stood backstage, excitement flowing through her blood. The sounds of the crowd rang in her ears, and she took a deep breath, calming herself. This was it—the moment she had worked so hard for. Suni told herself to enjoy every second and to trust in her training. She was prepared to shine bright in Tokyo.

A Performance for the Ages

When Suni Lee stepped onto the competition floor, the world held its breath. The moment was

Suni Lee

monumental—a result of years of commitment, sacrifice, and unshakable drive. As she prepared to perform her dances, Suni felt a mix of joy and jitters, but she turned those feelings into her performance, determined to give it her all. Suni's first event was the uneven bars, a sport that needed accuracy and power. As she climbed onto the device, the crowd erupted in applause, their cheers ringing through the venue. With each move, Suni showed her amazing ability and ease. Her routine was a perfect mix of tough elements and smooth changes, showing her unique style. As she performed her dismount, the crowd broke into cheers, recognizing the greatness of her performance. Suni felt a rush of energy and confidence—this was just the beginning.

Next up was the balance beam, an extremely difficult event that needed both skill and calm.

Suni Lee

Suni took a moment to collect herself before going onto the beam, telling herself of all the hard work she had put in. The beam was only four inches wide, but Suni's attention was steady. She completed her routine with accuracy, each action showing her years of training. When she landed her dismount, the crowd roared once again, and Suni knew she had given another strong performance.

The dance exercise was the final event, and it was here that Suni truly let her personality show. The music played, and she began her act with infectious energy and excitement. Suni's moves were smooth and strong, showing her strength and artistic expression. The crowd was captivated, and Suni could feel their energy powering her show. As she made her final pass, the audience exploded in cheers, and she knew she had left everything on the floor. With each

Suni Lee

exercise finished, Suni felt a wave of feelings wash over her. The hard work, the sacrifices, and the constant pursuit of greatness had all led to this moment. As she left the competition floor, Suni was filled with a sense of achievement, knowing that she had given her best effort.

The scores were collected, and Suni watched the results with bated breath. When the final scores were given, the crowd broke into cheers as Suni understood she had achieved something historic—she was the new Olympic winner. Overwhelmed with joy, Suni celebrated with her coworkers, realizing that this success was not just hers alone, but a testament to their combined hard work and support.

Suni's effort in Tokyo would go down in history as one of the most memorable in Olympic gymnastics. She had not only won the gold award but had also inspired countless young players around the world to follow their dreams. Suni Lee truly shone bright in Tokyo, showing that hard work and drive can lead to amazing success.

The Gold Medal Moment

The moment Suni Lee stood atop the platform, wrapped in her gold award, was a sight that would be etched in the minds of those who watched it. As the national anthem played, Suni reflected on her great journey—the sacrifices made, the difficulties faced, and the constant support from her family, teachers, and friends. This was the conclusion of a childhood dream, and the feelings rushed over her.

Receiving the gold award was a strange experience for Suni. As the medal was put around her neck, she felt a rush of pride and joy.

Suni Lee

This moment marked years of hard work and dedication, and she was overcome with thanks for everyone who had backed her along the way. Suni thought of her family, who had been her biggest fans, always urging her to chase her goals, no matter the hurdles. Their unwavering belief in her fueled her drive and gave her the strength to endure. As Suni looked out at the crowd, she could see the joy on the faces of her friends and trainers. They had worked hard alongside her, and this win was a shared success. Suni felt a deep sense of connection to her fellow athletes, understanding that they had all pushed each other to hit new heights. In that moment, she understood the true meaning of teamwork and camaraderie—a tie that stretched beyond competition. With the weight of the gold award sitting on her chest, Suni was filled with a feeling of duty. She knew that her win was not just a personal success; it was an example for young dancers everywhere. Suni wanted to show them that dreams are possible through hard work and determination. She hoped that her story would motivate others to believe in themselves and follow their interests, no matter the obstacles they may face.

As she stepped down from the platform, Suni was met with hugs and compliments from her friends and trainers. The joy and pride in their faces reflected her own, making a moment of pure happiness. The gold award was a sign of their joint trip, a testament to the commitment and resolve of everyone involved. Suni felt grateful to share this experience with her gymnastics family. In the days following her historic performance, Suni became a source of hope and inspiration for endless fans around the world. Media sites praised her successes, and she

Suni Lee

found herself in the spotlight as she shared her story. Suni welcomed the chance to connect with others, using her platform to promote the value of hard work, grit, and staying true to oneself. The gold medal moment was more than just an award; it was a sign of Suni's amazing journey and the effect she had made on the world of gymnastics. She had proven that with desire, drive, and support, goals could become a reality. As Suni continued to shine bright, she stayed dedicated to her craft, knowing that this was only the beginning of her journey as an athlete and a role mode

CHAPTER 7: MORE THAN JUST A GYMNAST

A Role Model for Young Athletes

Suni Lee's journey to Olympic glory turned her into a role model for young players everywhere. As she stood on the platform, wrapped in her gold award, she became a sign of perseverance, determination, and the chase of dreams. Her story connected with countless children and hopeful gymnasts who looked up to her as an example of what hard work and drive could achieve. Suni's effect went far beyond her great sports achievements. She became an inspiration for kids from all families, especially those who faced difficulties similar to her own. Growing up as a first-generation Hmong American, Suni managed cultural standards, language hurdles, and social pressures while following her love for gymnastics. Her ability to beat these challenges encouraged many young players, showing them that with perseverance and determination, they could achieve their dreams, no matter their circumstances.

Through social media and public events, Suni actively interacted with her fans, sharing bits of her life as an athlete and the lessons she learned along the way. She often stressed the importance of staying true to oneself and never giving up, urging young players to accept their uniqueness and follow their interests. Suni's sincerity and relatability made her a popular figure, as she shared not only her wins but also her challenges, creating a sense of connection with her audience. Suni's job as a guide went beyond her words. She often joined youth gymnastics camps, where she would share her skills and provide support to young gymnasts. These conversations helped her to connect with prospective players on a human level, motivating them to think big and work hard. Suni's desire to give back to the sport that had changed her life showed her dedication to supporting the next generation of gymnasts. Moreover, Suni's story promoted differences in sports. By openly expressing her Hmong background, she became a voice for overlooked groups in gymnastics and beyond. Suni's success sent a strong message to young players from different backgrounds that they could achieve greatness in any area. She became an advocate for diversity and participation, encouraging kids to accept their identities while following their interests.

As she continued her journey as a role model, Suni Lee stayed committed to using her position for good change. She aimed to inspire not just future gymnasts but also all young athletes who dared to dream big. Suni's memory as a role model was not just about her awards and honors but about the ongoing effect she had on the lives of countless young people, inspiring them to reach for the stars and believe in themselves.

Advocacy and Social Impact

With her renewed fame, Suni Lee accepted the chance to fight for important social problems. As an Olympic winner, she understood the stage she had to effect change and raise awareness about topics close to her heart. Suni became open about mental health, racial equality, and the value of helping disadvantaged groups, using her power to make a real effect.One of the major problems Suni worked on was mental health in sports. The pressure players face can often lead to mental health challenges, and Suni freely shared her experiences with worry and the importance of valuing mental well-being. She stressed that it was okay to seek help and that mental health should be treated with the same importance as physical health. Suni's openness about her problems connected with many young players who felt the load of demands. By sharing her story, she helped reduce the stigma surrounding mental health, pushing others to value self-care and reach out for support when needed.

Suni also became a champion for racial equality and participation in sports. As a Hmong American, she faced unique hurdles in her journey, and she used her position to address issues of diversity and equality. Suni spoke out against injustice and pushed for the participation of neglected groups in gymnastics and other sports. Her commitment to these causes influenced many, urging players and fans to join the talk about equality and fairness in sports. In addition to fighting for mental health and racial equality, Suni Lee was committed to giving back to her community. She often joined in charitable events and projects aimed at helping youth programs, especially those focused on sports and education. Suni felt that giving opportunities to young people was important in helping them achieve their dreams. By participating in charity, she wanted to have a good effect on the lives of children and inspire them to achieve their goals. Suni's lobbying efforts went to promoting physical health and happiness. She frequently shared tips on healthy living and staying busy, stressing the value of exercise and a balanced lifestyle. Through her social media outlets and public speaking events, Suni encouraged her fans to value their health and well-being, showing how exercise could motivate them to lead meaningful lives. Suni Lee's commitment to campaigning and social effect showed her understanding of the duty that came with her success. She used her position to create important talks and inspire change, showing that sports could be strong speakers for progress. As she continued her journey, Suni stayed committed to making a difference in the world, leaving a legacy that exceeded her successes as a dancer.

A Lasting Legacy

Suni Lee's effect on gymnastics and society will be felt for years to come, producing a long legacy that stretches far beyond her awards and titles. Her story serves as a testament to the power of hard work, drive, and grit, inspiring generations of young players to dream big and continue in the face of obstacles. Suni's impact includes not only her successes but also her dedication to campaigning and making a good change in the world.

As Suni continues her career in gymnastics, she has become a source of hope and inspiration for young athletes. Her journey, marked by dedication and grit, shows that greatness can be achieved through hard work and an unshakable confidence in oneself. Young gymnasts around the world look up to her as a role model, seeing in her the embodiment of the ideals of resilience and drive. Suni's story urges them to follow their dreams relentlessly, telling them that hurdles can be overcome with commitment and desire.

Suni Lee

Suni's impact goes beyond the sports community. Her support for mental health, social equality, and inclusion in sports has started important talks and inspired action. By using her platform to raise awareness about these problems, Suni has become a voice for change, encouraging others to take a stand for what is right. Her commitment to social justice connects with many, showing that sports can be strong agents of good change in their communities and beyond. The effect of Suni's success is also visible in the growing interest in gymnastics among young players. Her journey has motivated many to take up the sport, leading to a new crop of gymnasts eager to follow in her path. Suni's success has helped bring gymnastics into the spotlight, showing the beauty and skill of the sport. As young athletes watch her fight and achieve, they are inspired to train hard, improve their skills, and follow their dreams of becoming gymnasts.

Furthermore, Suni's position as a Hmong American star has opened doors for greater variety in gymnastics. Her success has paved the way for more players from underrepresented backgrounds to follow their dreams in the sport. By breaking barriers and destroying assumptions, Suni has shown that ability knows no limits, encouraging young players from all walks of life to accept their uniqueness and aim for greatness.

In the years to come, Suni Lee's influence will continue to encourage and strengthen future generations. Her story serves as a lesson that success is not simply measured by awards or recognition, but by the effect one can have on others. As Suni continues to shine brightly, she leaves behind a legacy of hope, courage, and

Suni Lee

inspiration, showing that with hard work, desire, and a commitment to making a difference, anyone can achieve greatness.

CHAPTER8: THE ROAD AHEAD

Continuing the Gymnastics Journey

As Suni Lee looks to the future, her gymnastics journey is far from over.her recent success at the Tokyo Olympics, Suni has not only solidified her place in gymnastics history but also set her sights on further achievements. The world of gymnastics is always changing, with new techniques and skills appearing, and Suni is dedicated to staying at the head of this dynamic sport. She is committed to honing her skills, improving her routines, and planning for future challenges, including national titles and possible foreign events.

Suni's training program stays intense, as she focuses on keeping peak physical fitness and learning new elements in her exercises. Under the direction of her teachers, she tries creative combos that can improve her displays and keep her competitive. Suni knows that gymnastics demands not only strength and flexibility but also imagination and skill. She welcomes the task of continually pushing her limits, knowing that every practice session is a chance to learn and grow.

In addition to her mechanical skills, Suni stresses the value of mental planning. Competing at the top level can be mentally tiring, and Suni is highly aware of the need to build mental strength. She participates in meditation methods, positive mantras, and relaxation practices to help her stay focused and strong during contests. By valuing her mental health, Suni aims to approach her future acts with clarity and calm, ready to face any difficulties that may appear.

As she continues her gymnastics journey, Suni also wants to inspire her fellow dancers to strive for greatness. She joins in classes and camps, sharing her experiences and thoughts with prospective players. Suni believes in the value of mentoring and community, and she is enthusiastic about helping others manage their gymnastics paths. By creating a nurturing environment, she pushes young gymnasts to follow their goals and enjoy the joys of the sport. Suni's commitment to gymnastics also goes beyond her personal goals. She hopes to push for greater chances in the sport, especially for young players from varied backgrounds. By using her platform to support equality and accessibility in gymnastics, Suni aims to ensure that every child, regardless of their background, has the chance to join in the sport and reach their full potential.

The road ahead for Suni Lee is filled with exciting prospects. With her dedication to greatness and her love for gymnastics, she is set to leave a lasting mark on the sport. Whether it's fighting on the world stage or teaching the next generation of gymnasts, Suni's journey is just starting, and she is determined to make every moment count.

Expanding Her Influence Beyond Gymnastics

Suni Lee's effect goes far beyond her successes in gymnastics. With her rise to fame, she has the chance to affect various parts of society, including young culture, mental health understanding, and inclusion in sports. As she navigates this new stage in her life, Suni is

Suni Lee

committed to leveraging her position to fight for important causes and spark positive change. One place where Suni hopes to make a change is in mental health support. Her own experiences with worry and pressure have given her useful insights into the importance of mental well-being, especially for young sports. Suni understands that the challenges players face can often go ignored, leading to mental health problems that can affect their success and general quality of life. By sharing her story and promoting talks around mental health, Suni wants to encourage others to value their well-being and seek help when needed. Suni is also dedicated to raising understanding about the value of variety and participation in sports. As a Hmong American athlete, she knows the importance of exposure and inclusivity for neglected groups. By pushing for better inclusion in gymnastics and other sports, Suni aims to encourage young players from various backgrounds to follow their interests without fear or limitation. She thinks that everyone should have the chance to join in sports and that diversity improves the athletic community.

In addition to her lobbying activities, Suni Lee is considering possibilities in the media and entertainment business. Her charm, energy, and relatability have made her a beloved figure among fans, and she is keen to connect with a bigger audience. Suni sees engaging in television shows, films, and public speaking events that highlight her journey and the importance of grit, commitment, and self-acceptance. Through these platforms, she wants to encourage others and share important life lessons that stretch beyond gymnastics.

Suni's future may also include partnerships with brands and groups that match her morals. By working with businesses that support health, fitness, and inclusion, Suni can spread her message and reach a wider audience. Whether it's through product ads or community projects, she aims to use her impact to support good change and encourage young players to chase their dreams. The road ahead for Suni Lee is bright, as she welcomes the chance to grow her impact beyond gymnastics. With a commitment to mental health support, inclusion, and inspiring the next generation, Suni is determined to leave a long impact that speaks with people from all walks of life. Her story is a testament to the power of hard work and the effect one person can have on the world.

Education and Personal Growth

In addition to her sports interests, Suni Lee is truly committed to her schooling and personal growth. As she continues to succeed in gymnastics, Suni sees the value of combining her sports career with her school efforts. Education has always been a focus for her, and she thinks that knowledge and personal growth are important components of a well-rounded life. Suni has voiced her desire to pursue higher education, and she is exploring choices that fit with her hobbies and goals. Whether it's studying sports management, psychology, or another area, Suni knows that her education can open doors for her future efforts. She aims to use her stage to emphasize the value of education for young players, supporting them to achieve their academic goals alongside their sports ambitions.

Suni Lee

Suni thinks that schooling offers important skills and information that can help people throughout their lives, both inside and outside of sports. In addition to traditional schooling, Suni is dedicated to personal progress and self-improvement. She eagerly seeks chances to learn and build new skills, whether it's through classes, mentoring, or events outside of gymnastics. Suni knows that growth is a lifelong process, and she welcomes the obstacles and lessons that come her way. By engaging in her personal growth, Suni aims to become the best version of herself, both as an athlete and as an individual.

Suni's trip also stresses the value of endurance and flexibility. In the ever-changing world of sports and life, she understands that failures and difficulties are part of the process. Instead of shying away from problems, Suni approaches them with a growth attitude, viewing hurdles as chances for learning and growth. This viewpoint not only improves her success as a dancer but also prepares her for the challenges of life beyond sports.

Moreover, Suni aims to use her experiences to teach and help other young players navigate their journeys. She knows that the road to success can be difficult, and she is enthusiastic about sharing her insights and giving advice to those who seek it. By creating a sense of community and support among young players, Suni hopes to inspire them to believe in themselves and follow their dreams boldly. As Suni Lee looks to the future, her commitment to education and personal growth stays steadfast. With a focus on intellectual interests, ongoing learning, and teaching others, she is motivated to build a well-rounded and rewarding life beyond

Suni Lee

gymnastics. Suni's story is a lesson that success is not only defined by sports achievements but also by the effect one can have on their community and the world around them.

CONCLUSION: THE LEGACY OF SUNI LEE

Suni Lee's memory is based on her amazing journey and the power of resilience. From a young age, Suni faced numerous difficulties that could have stopped her from following her dreams. Growing up as a Hmong American in a society where visibility was limited, she managed cultural hurdles and social standards while improving her gymnastics skills. Despite the odds stacked against her, Suni's unwavering drive drove her desire to succeed. Her story serves as a reference to the idea that hard work and perseverance can lead to amazing success. Suni's trip was not without its struggles; she faced failures and losses along the way. However, each task only increased her

Suni Lee

determination. Suni learned early on that failure is not the end but rather a chance for growth and change. With every fall, she rose stronger, displaying her grit and drive to succeed. Suni's experiences connect with countless individuals, especially young players who may feel defeated in the face of hardship. She represents the idea that failures are merely stepping stones to success. Through her story, Suni pushes others to accept their obstacles and continue toward their goals. She pushes young people to adopt a growth attitude, telling them that every mistake is a chance to learn and. Moreover, Suni's resolve goes beyond gymnastics. She pushes for mental health understanding, stressing the value of grit in handling life's stresses. Her openness about her battles with worry and self-doubt provides a realistic view for many, telling them that it's okay to seek help and support. By sharing her experiences, Suni encourages others to value their mental well-being and develop strength in their lives.Suni Lee's impact is a strong lesson that perseverance is not just about achieving personal goals; it's about inspiring others to push through their difficulties. Her story will continue to inspire generations to come, inspiring individuals to accept their journeys and follow their interests with unwavering drive. Suni's effect surpasses gymnastics; she is a sign of hope and grit, showing that with hard work and determination, anything is possible.

Another important part of Suni Lee's impact is her role as a fighter of representation. As a Hmong American gymnast, Suni broke limits and shattered stereotypes within a sport that has long lacked diversity. Her success on the world stage brought attention to the value of inclusion in gymnastics and inspired countless young athletes from varied backgrounds to follow their dreams.

Suni's rise to fame shows the need for inclusion in sports. She has become a voice for overlooked groups, pushing for greater exposure and chances for players from all walks of life. Suni's journey connects deeply with young people who may feel ignored or forgotten in their goals. By getting Olympic gold and becoming a role model, she sends a strong message that ability knows no limits and that anyone can achieve greatness regardless of their background. Her influence is not just about her athletic successes; it stretches to the talks surrounding diversity and inclusion in sports. Suni's success has sparked important conversations about inclusion, pushing groups and institutions to address the need for different participation at all levels of

Suni Lee

gymnastics. Her position in the sport opens the way for more young athletes from different backgrounds to follow in her footsteps, breaking down walls and expanding the meaning of what it means to be a gymnast.Suni Lee's impact as a champion of inclusion goes beyond her achievements. She embodies the view that everyone should have the chance to join in sports and be honored for their special backgrounds. By using her platform to fight for diversity and tolerance, Suni pushes young players to accept their identities and follow their interests without fear or restriction.Her journey serves as a light of hope for those who may feel disheartened by social standards. Suni pushes young people to think big and understand that their backgrounds and experiences improve the games they love. As she continues to shine strongly in the world of gymnastics, Suni Lee

Suni Lee

leaves behind a legacy that supports inclusion, tolerance, and the celebration of variety in all its forms.Suni Lee's memory is a deep source of motivation for future generations of sports and thinkers alike. As she continues to grow as an athlete and champion, her story serves as a guiding light for young people following their interests, whether in gymnastics or any other area. Suni's story shows that success is not just about individual awards; it's about the impact one can have on others and the memories they leave behind. Her amazing story from a young girl training in her garden to an Olympic gold winner captures the spirit of determination, hard work, and resilience. Young athletes watching Suni compete see not just a skilled dancer, but a role model who represents perseverance and authenticity. They watch her commitment to her work, her ability to beat hurdles, and her dedication to uplifting others. Suni's story urges them to believe in their skills and to aim for greatness, regardless of the obstacles they may face. Suni's impact goes beyond sports; she pushes young people to accept their uniqueness and use their talents for change. Her support for mental health understanding, variety, and tolerance urges future generations to value well-being and fight for their communities. Suni's openness about her problems serves as a lesson that it's okay to ask for help and that sensitivity is a strength. She encourages young people to be real, to accept their identities, and to use their experiences to inspire others.

Moreover, Suni Lee's influence goes far beyond gymnastics. She represents the idea that anyone can be a change-maker in their way. Whether through sports, art, politics, or any other interest, Suni's journey pushes people to follow their dreams relentlessly and to boost those around them. Her memory urges young people to find their voices, stand up for what they believe in, and make a good change in the world. As Suni Lee continues her journey, her impact will surely inspire generations to come. Young players will look up to her as a sign of hope and determination, knowing that greatness is possible through hard work, grit, and a commitment to making a difference. Suni's story serves as a strong reminder that each person has the potential to leave a permanent effect on their community and inspire others to chase their dreams.

Suni Lee

FUN FACTS ABOUT SUNI LEE

Did You Know?

Olympic History Maker: Suni Lee made history by becoming the first Hmong American to play in the Olympics. Her win at the 2020 Tokyo Olympics, where she won gold in the women's individual all-around gymnastics competition, was a groundbreaking moment for inclusion in sports.

Multi-Talented Athlete: Besides gymnastics, Suni is a skilled dancer and has shown interest in other sports, including dancing and track. Her diverse sports background adds to her amazing speed and grace in gymnastics.

Suni Lee

Inspired by Family: Suni has often praised her family, especially her father, for backing her dreams. Her dad, who was a successful athlete in his own right, pushed her to pursue gymnastics, and they have shared a close bond throughout her journey.

Social Media Sensation: Suni is quite famous on social media, especially on sites like Instagram and TikTok. She often shares behind-the-scenes glimpses of her training, personal life, and fun challenges, making her a relatable figure for fans and ambitious gymnasts.

Pursuing Education: While succeeding in gymnastics, Suni also values her education. After the Olympics, she committed to joining Auburn University, where she plans to continue her gymnastics career while focusing on her

Suni Lee

studies, showing her commitment to both sports and schoolwork.

GLOSSARY

Gymnastics Terms to Know

All-Around: A competition where a gymnast participates in multiple events (usually four for women: vault, uneven bars, balance beam, and floor exercise) and their points are mixed to determine a total rating.

Balance Beam: A narrow, raised device that gymnasts perform exercises on, needing strength, balance, and accuracy. It is one of the events in women's artistic gymnastics.

Flair: A skill performed on the pommel horse or floor that includes the gymnast moving their legs in a circular motion while keeping balance and control.

Vault: An event in which gymnasts run down a track and jump onto a springboard to perform amazing skills over a vaulting table. It takes speed, power, and skill.

Routine: A set of moves and skills performed by a gymnast on an object. Each performance is scored based on challenge, technique, and creativity.

Dismount: The final move of a performance where the gymnast leaves the equipment, resting on their feet. Dismounts are often complicated and require accuracy to score well.

Tumbling: A series of acrobatic moves made on the floor, including flips, spins, and rolls. Tumbling is an important part of floor workout routines.

. **Split Leap**: A movement where a gymnast jumps into the air with one leg extended forward and the other backward, forming a "split" pose. It displays elasticity and height.

Chalk: A magnesium carbonate powder used by gymnasts to improve their grip on devices like the bars and rings, helping to avoid slides during exercises.

Scoring: The review process in gymnastics events where judges rate a gymnast's performance based on difficulty (the value of skills performed) and execution (how well each skill is performed). The total score is taken from the sum of these ratings.

Acknowledgments

In this part, Suni Lee offers her deep thanks to the people and groups who have played a major role in her road to becoming an Olympic winner. Family and **Friends**: First and foremost, I want to thank my family, who have been my constant support system. To my parents, thank you for your constant love, support, and sacrifices. You believed in me from day one and always pushed me to reach for my dreams. To my brothers, your fun and support kept me centered and driven during the hardest times. I couldn't have done it without you all.

Coaches and Mentors: A special thank you goes to my teachers, who led me every step of the way. Your knowledge, kindness, and support have changed me not only as an athlete but also as a person. Each lesson you taught me, whether about sports or life, has been priceless. I am grateful for your trust in my abilities and for helping me improve my skills to fight at the top levels.

Team USA: I want to show my thanks to my friends and everyone connected with Team USA.

Your unity and energy produced a setting that made training and fighting a joy. Together, we did great things, and I am glad to be a part of such an incredible team.

Fans and Supporters: To all my friends and followers, thank you for cheering me on throughout my trip. Your support and love have fueled my desire for gymnastics. Knowing that I have such a determined support system behind me has been a great driver.

Community and Heritage: I also want to recognize my Hmong community, who have inspired me and reminded me of the value of participation and hard work. Your pride in my successes encourages me to continue pushing limits and breaking barriers.

Mental Health Advocates: Lastly, I want to thank those who fight for mental health understanding in sports. Your efforts to destigmatize mental health problems have pushed me to be open about my own difficulties, helping me to grow stronger both on and off the mat.

Together, you have all played a key role in my journey, and I am truly grateful for your support. Thank you for believing in me and for helping me shine brightly in my gymnastics career.

Made in the USA
Las Vegas, NV
14 April 2025